SPARKLING *Cake* DESIGNS

by Karen Davies

To Amy, Happy 18th Birthday,
with all my love.

Magic Sparkles have been used on all the cakes in this book. They are edible and safe to use on any cake decorating from fairy cakes to wedding cakes. They can be used on cakes, sweets, chocolates or desserts for a special touch.

Use straight from the pot or grind down to a finer glitter. To do this either leave in the pot and stir with a teaspoon handle or use a pestle and mortar. To attach to cakes the surface should be tacky not wet – if too wet they will dissolve. Always sprinkle over greaseproof paper so any excess can be returned to the pot. Edible glue is ideal although you can use water or alcohol. Their appearance is enhanced by good lighting - halogen or spotlights work well.

How To Use The Size Guide

On any instructions for modelling in this book I have used the Cel Cakes Size Guide. This should make it easier to produce proportioned figures. To achieve the correct size, the ball of paste should sit in the correct hole (size below it) with 1/3 out of the bottom and 2/3 out of the top (this does not apply to the smallest sizes). You will then have approximately the correct size ball of paste to shape.

Recipes

Modelling Paste

Either:- $1/2$ sugarpaste $1/2$ flower paste kneaded together, or knead 5ml (1tsp) of gum tragacanth into 225g (8ozs) sugarpaste and leave for 8 hours, or knead 5ml (1tsp) Tylo (CMC) powder into 225g (8ozs) sugarpaste.

Mexican Paste

Mix together 225g (8ozs) of icing sugar and 3 level teaspoons of gum tragacanth. Add 25ml (5tsp) of cold water (taken from tap). Mix together, turnout and knead well. Store in a plastic bag and a sealed container for 6-8 hours to mature. The paste will feel very hard but will soften up easily. Break off small pieces and soften in your fingers. Matured paste will freeze.

Royal Icing

Place 30ml (6 level tsp) of merriwhite in a mixing bowl and gradually add 5tbs cold water mixing with a wooden spoon until free from lumps. Add 225g (8ozs) of icing sugar and mix until smooth. Add 110g (4ozs) of icing sugar and then add the rest gradually until the correct consistency is reached. Beat well for approximately 5 minutes. Store in the fridge in an airtight container. Should keep for 4 weeks.

Softened Sugarpaste

Place the amount of sugarpaste you want to soften in a bowl. Chop up roughly and then gradually add drops of cold water. Break down with a fork or a spoon and mix until smooth and lump free. Continue until required consistency is reached. The first time you do this, be careful not to add too much water too soon. It softens quickly.

Edible Glue

This is easily made with 1 part Tylo (CMC) powder to 25-30 parts water. Place the powder in a bottle or jar that has a lid. Add the water, replace the lid and shake. There will be thick creamy white pieces in the water. They will dissolve and the liquid will become clear by the following day.

NOTE: ANY SPECIAL EQUIPMENT USED HAS A SUPPLIER CODE. FOR EXAMPLE – SIZE GUIDE (CC) – SUPPLIER CEL CAKES. SEE ACKNOWLEDGMENTS PAGE 37

Anniversary Cake

25cm x 20cm (10in x 8in) Oval marzipanned rich fruit cake, 36cm x 31cm (14in x 12in) oval cake drum, 1.3kg (3lb) sugarpaste, Mexican paste (p1), sugar glue (p1), piping gel or Scintillo blue and silver (SK), Trex, isopropyl alcohol.

Squires Kitchen Paste Colours:
Gentian, Marigold, Rose, Chestnut, Black.

Powder Colours: Snowflake Lustre, Rose, Silver, Berberis, Black.

Magic Sparkles: White, Hint of Blue, Yellow, all ground finer (p1).

Squares embosser (from Patchwork Squares set, PC), Glass cutter (from Bottle & Glass set, PC), Duck (from Nursery set PC), Dresden tool, no.1 & 2 piping nozzles, frilling stick / Mouth tool (JEM), 1/2in plain curve crimper, Straight frill cutter no.3 from set 1 (FMM), 3cm (1in) circle cutter, non-stick rolling pin & board.

1 Place cake on board and cover with sugarpaste. Ice board and crimp edge.

2 Emboss square grid so that the bottom line is halfway down cake. Mark tiles on floor with a Dresden tool by spreading out the lines from the wall tiles starting at each side and then evenly between.

3 Grease a non-stick board and the glass cutter with Trex. Roll out Mexican paste and cut out two glasses. Leave to dry. Colour a little Mexican paste yellow and cut out six ducks and six wings. Attach wings to ducks using sugar glue. Leave to dry.

4 Knead together 100g of sugarpaste and 25g of Mexican paste. Make a paper template from greaseproof paper of the sides of the cake. The width of the template should be 4cm. Roll paste out thinly and cut out a long straight piece of paste using the template. Keep the bottom edge straight but trim the top edge with the frill cutter. Brush lower half of the cake side with water, roll up border and unroll around the cake. Brush border with water, leave until tacky then tilt the cake slightly and sprinkle the blue sparkles over.

5 Colour 75g of sugarpaste pale blue and cut out bath (p35). Roll a long sausage of paste and flatten slightly for top edge. Attach with sugar glue. Shape bath feet and mark with a Dresden tool. Attach with sugar glue.

6 Colour the left over paste from the straight frill using rose and chestnut to get a flesh colour. Roll out thinly and cut two opposite bodies (p35). Place in bath securing with sugar glue. Roll out paste twice as thick and cut out two heads using the circle cutter. Attach and emboss mouth using the mouth tool. Dip a cocktail stick into black paste colour and mark eyes. Position glasses, securing with sugar glue. Roll small balls of flesh coloured paste into oval shapes. Attach over glass stem. Mark fingers with a knife and nails with a no.2 piping nozzle. Colour a little royal icing and pipe on hair with a no.1 or 2 nozzle. Brush cheeks with a little rose powder colour.

7 Attach pieces of sugarpaste a few at a time for bubbles. Quickly tap a no.1 piping nozzle all over. Place bubbles in bath, on floor and around cake.

8 Model a tap, attach to end of bath. When dry paint with silver powder colour mixed with isopropyl alcohol.

9 Brush Snowflake lustre over tiles, bath and bubbles. Brush bubbles lightly with water then sprinkle with white sparkles.

10 For the water, use blue and silver Scintillo or colour piping gel with Snowflake and blue or silver powder. Place in piping bags. Pipe drips to edge of bath. Pipe varying shades of gel around board using a brush to spread and blend.

11 Paint ducks eyes black, beaks orange, then cover with yellow sparkles. Push into iced board at intervals around cake.

12 Pipe a message using a no.1 nozzle and royal icing. When dry paint silver.

Fairy Teddy

20cm(8in) Square marzipanned rich fruit cake, 28cm(11in) drum board, 900g (2lb) Shell Pink Regalice, 450g(1lb) modelling paste (p1), a little Mexican paste (p1), sugar glue (p1), Trex.

Squires Kitchen Paste Colours:
Rose, Bulrush, Black.

Powder Colours: Rose, Snowflake.

Magic Sparkles: Pink, Hint of Pink, White, all ground finer (p1).

Straight frill cutter set 2, no.7, (FMM), garrett frill cutter, small blossom cutter (FMM), Butterfly cutter (PC), Frilling / mouth tool (JEM), no.1 piping nozzle, ball tool, size guide (CC).

1 Place cake on board and cover with shell pink sugarpaste. Ice board.

2 Divide modelling paste in two. Keep 1/2 for teddy. Split the other 1/2 into quarters. Colour 2/4 pink, 1/4 pale pink, 1/4 leave white.

3 Roll out the pink modelling paste thinly to cut out the straight frill. Trim to approximately 1.5cm using a ruler and a cutting wheel. Attach around the base of the cake with sugarglue – taking care not to stretch the frill out of shape. Roll out pink modelling paste again and cut out the same frill to attach to the board.

4 Roll out the pale pink paste and this time cut both edges with the frill cutter and attach directly above the pink frill around the cake. Repeat with the white paste attaching above the pale pink frill.

5 Grind down each of the magic sparkles finer (p1). Brush sugar glue thinly over the white frill, tilt the cake, and while still tacky, sprinkle on the white sparkles. Repeat with the hint of pink over the pale pink frill, then the pink sparkles over the pink frills on the cake and board.

6 Soften a little pink sugarpaste (p1) and pipe a plain shell around base of cake.

7 Shape the teddy's body – teardrop / pearshape, from a no.15 size piece (using the size guide) of shell pink sugarpaste. Colour 60g (2 1/2ozs) of modelling paste light brown. Shape two legs each from a size 8 piece of paste and two feet each a size 11. Attach together and to body with sugar glue. Attach to centre of cake.

8 The skirt is made from garrett frills. Cut out two pink frills in modelling paste and frill with the frilling tool. Paint a little sugar glue around lower body and place frills over (as you place frills over body, position each one slightly higher than the previous and trim off any excess at the back). Repeat with two pale pink and then two white, finishing at waist level.

9 Shape two arms each from a size 8 piece of brown modelling paste. Keep the arms thinner at the shoulder. Mark a seam down arms and a crease at the elbow with a knife. Attach with sugar glue.

10 Using the size guide, shape head from a size 13 ball of paste. Pinch head a little thinner at the eye area then mark seams with a knife. Attach head to body. Indent a mouth with the mouth tool. Dip the end of a cocktail stick into black paste colour then use to mark eyes. Roll a small ball of paste for the ears, indent with a ball tool then cut in half. Attach to head with sugar glue. Colour a small ball of modelling paste brown and attach for nose.

11 Colour Mexican paste pale pink. Grease a non-stick rolling board with Trex. Grease the butterfly cutter with Trex. Roll out Mexican paste thinly. Cut out the butterfly. Discard the body. Brush the wings thinly with sugar glue and cover with hint of pink sparkles. The wings should be attached after stage 12 before they are dry. This will enable them to bend to fit the bear.

12 Cut out 3 blossoms in pink Mexican paste and attach to bears head. Dust a little pink powder colour into ears, cheeks, onto feet and edge of skirt frills. Dust bear all over with Snowflake. Attach wings with sugar glue.

20cm (8in) Heart Shaped marzipanned rich fruit cake, 31cm (12in) drum board, 900g (2lb) sugarpaste, Mexican paste (p1), sugar glue (p1), isopropyl alcohol, Trex.

Squires Kitchen Paste Colours: **Rose, Gentian, Violet.**

Powder Colour: **Snowflake, Silver.**

Magic Sparkles: **Hint of Pink, White (both ground finer p1).**

Butterfly cutter (PC), Large heart cutter 55mm (FMM), small blossom from blossom cutter set (FMM), heart cutter 13mm from small heart cutter set (FMM), 2 bunches each of crystal flowers and diamantes on silver stems (CCB or Culpitt), fine paintbrush.

1 Place cake on board and cover both cake and board together with sugarpaste. Emboss the top of the cake immediately with large heart cutters.

2 Colour 50g Mexican paste pink, plus two small pieces – one lilac and the other gentian.

3 Roll out pink Mexican paste to approximately a (1/4in) thick and cut out two large hearts. Smooth the cut edges with your finger to give a smoother edge. Attach to embossed hearts with sugar glue.

4 Grease a non-stick rolling board and the butterfly cutter with Trex. Roll out blue Mexican paste thinly and cut out approximately 16 butterflies. Attach to the cake with sugar glue. Repeat with pink Mexican paste for 22 hearts and lilac paste for 25 small blossoms.

5 Mix a little silver powder colour with isopropyl alcohol and paint fine antennae for each butterfly.

6 Dust the large hearts on top of cake with snowflake lustre.

7 Brush the small hearts, butterflies and blossoms with sugar glue. When just 'tacky' sprinkle with white Magic Sparkles.

8 Brush a little sugar glue on cake around large hearts and sprinkle with hint of pink sparkles.

9 Undo the diamante and flowers from their bunches. Twist together into a long band to fit around base of cake. Twist ends together at the back of cake to hold together.

20cm (8in) Round marzipanned rich fruit cake, 28cm (11in) round cake drum, 900g (2lb) sugarpaste, flower paste (SK), sugar glue (p1), piping gel – or Scintillo blue and silver (SK).

Squires Kitchen Paste Colours:
Gentian, Mint, Marigold, Black.

Squires Kitchen Powder Colours:
Snowflake Lustre, Rose.

Magic Sparkles: Yellow, Hint of Green, both ground finer (p1).

Large Daisy Cutter 7cm (PME), size guide (CC), no.3 paintbrush.

1 Colour 700g (1¹/²lb) sugarpaste blue. Place cake on board and cover with blue icing. Colour 110g (4ozs) sugarpaste green and use to ice board.

2 Roll out flower paste and cut out two daisies. Stick together with sugar glue. If you don't have a former, make a foil 'cup' to dry flower in. Colour a little flower paste yellow, roll a ball, flatten slightly and attach to centre with sugar glue. Leave to dry.

3 Using the size guide, roll a size 12 ball of sugar paste. Pinch the top and flatten slightly to give a pear shape. Attach with sugar glue so neck will be at the centre of the cake. Roll a size 9 for the head. Flatten slightly and attach.

4 Dip a cocktail stick into black paste colour and mark eyes.

5 Make two wings each from a size 7 ball of sugarpaste. Attach with sugar glue.

6 Colour a little sugar paste pale yellow. Roll two very thin sausages of paste for legs. Use a size 7 ball of paste for each foot. Attach with sugar glue. Mould a beak from a size 6. Leave to dry.

7 Soften a small piece of white sugarpaste (p1). Place in a piping bag and pipe small amounts on to duck. Use a damp paintbrush to brush into place and give duck a 'fluffy' appearance. Be careful not to touch the black eyes. Attach beak while brushed paste is still soft.

8 Take a size 6 ball of green sugarpaste and roll long and thin for the flower stem. Cut so a small piece can be attached below wing and a longer piece above.

9 Soften remaining green sugarpaste with water. Place in a piping bag and pipe small sections around base of cake. Using a damp paintbrush, brush icing up

cake and on to board to resemble grass. Brush a little sugar glue over grass and cover with hint of green sparkles.

10 Dust edge of daisy petals with rose powder colour. Dust daisy and duck with Snowflake Lustre. Brush daisy centre with sugar glue and cover with yellow Magic Sparkles. Attach daisy to cake using sugar glue.

11 Colour a little piping gel with Snowflake lustre and blue in different shades. Place in piping bags and pipe small raindrops and a puddle under the duck.

12 Pipe some small blossoms on grass and iced board.

Rose Birthday Cake

20cm (8in) Marzipanned rich fruit cake, 28cm (11in) drum board, 810g (1³⁄₄lb) sugarpaste, flower paste (SK), royal icing(p1), isopropyl alcohol.

Squires Kitchen paste colours: Violet, Rose, Mint.

Powder Colours: Silver, Snowflake.

Magic Sparkles: Hint of Lilac, Hint of Pink, White, all ground finer (p1).

Rose leaf cutter, no.2 piping nozzle, 4 stems of wired crystal beads, (³⁄₄in) double curve serrated crimper, rose leaf veiner, ball tool, pastry brush.

1 Place cake on board. Colour 700g sugarpaste pale lilac and ice cake.

2 Colour remaining sugarpaste pink and ice board. Crimp around board edge.

3 Colour some flower paste pink and green.

4 With the pink flower paste make a rose and leave to dry. Cut out 8 rose leaves from flower paste, vein, soften edges with a ball tool and leave to dry.

5 Make tiny leaves by rolling small balls of flower paste, pinching the top, flattening and making a centre vein with a knife. The rose buds are made from rolling small balls of paste into a sausage shape, flattening then rolling up tightly. Leave to dry.

6 Using a pastry brush, brush cake all over with a little water. Cover with the hint of lilac sparkles. Brush the icing on the board with the pastry brush and water then cover with the hint of pink sparkles.

7 Attach leaves and buds around the base of cake using royal icing.

8 Brush rose and leaves lightly with a little sugar glue and sprinkle white sparkles over. Arrange leaves, rose and wired crystals on top of cake and secure with royal icing.

9 With royal icing and a no 2 nozzle, pipe top edge of crimping around board edge. Pipe name or message on top of cake. Mix together silver powder and isopropyl alcohol and paint piped edge and name.

Heart Cake

20cm (8in) Round marzipanned rich fruit cake, 28cm (11in) drum board, 900g (2lb) shell pink Regalice, flower paste (SK), sugar glue (p1).

Squires Kitchen paste colour: Rose

Magic Sparkles: White, Pink and Hint of Pink.

5 White flower wires – size 22, heart cutter set (FMM), double curve ³/₄in serrated crimper, no.2 piping nozzle, posy pick, sponge pad.

1 Cut flower wires in half.

2 Roll out white flower paste thinly. Cut out six hearts of each size. Brush three small hearts with sugar glue. Place a wire on each keeping the tip approximately half way down the heart. Place a small heart directly on top of each.

3 Repeat with the medium size heart placing 1cm below the small heart, then with the large heart.

4 Colour some flower paste pale pink to match the shell pink and repeat the hearts on wires. Colour some flower paste a slightly darker pink and repeat again. Lay all hearts on wires flat to dry on a sponge pad.

5 Place cake on board and cover with shell pink regalice.

6 Using the heart cutters, emboss hearts randomly over cake.

7 Ice the board. Crimp board edge.

8 Soften a little sugarpaste (P1) and using the no.2 nozzle pipe a small plain shell around base of cake.

9 Fill the posy pick with pale pink flower paste and press into centre of the cake. Leave to dry slightly.

10 Grind each of the Magic Sparkles down finer (p1). Brush one side of the hearts on wires with sugar glue and cover with the appropriate sparkles. Leave to dry then turn over and repeat on other side. Leave to dry.

11 Paint hearts on cake with sugar glue and sprinkle with pink sparkles.

12 Push heart wires into paste in posy pick. Bend slightly to give a curved shape.

Blossom Cake

20cm (8in) Round marzipanned rich fruit cake, 28cm (11in) drum board, 810g (1³/₄lb) white sugarpaste, 110g (4ozs) flower paste (SK), royal icing (p1), sugar glue (p1).

Squires Kitchen paste colours: **Rose, Mint, Gentian, Violet, Marigold.**

Magic Sparkles: **White, Hint of Pink, Hint of green, Hint of Blue, Hint of Lilac – all ground finer (p1).**

Blossom cutters 3cm & 1cm (1in & ¹/₂ in) (FMM), rose leaf cutter 3cm (1in) (FMM), no.2 piping nozzle, ¹/₂in single curve serrated crimper, ball tool, non-stick rolling pin & board, sponge pad.

1 Colour 700g sugarpaste pale mint green.

2 Place cake on board and cover with the green icing. Ice the board with the remaining white sugarpaste. Crimp around edge of board. Leave to dry.

3 Divide flower paste into 5 equal pieces. Leave one piece white and colour the other pieces pale pink, green, blue and lilac.

4 Roll out green paste and cut out 40-50 leaves. Leave to dry. Cut out approximately 40 large blossoms in each colour. Place on a sponge pad and press a ball tool into the centre of each flower. Leave to dry. Cut out smaller blossoms in each colour. How many you will need depends on how close together they are placed on the cake. Cut out 20 of each colour at first and make more later if needed.

5 Brush the icing on board with sugar glue. Cover with white sparkles. Soften a little white sugarpaste (p1) and place in a piping bag with a no. 2 nozzle. Pipe a plain shell around base of cake.

6 Brush leaves with sugar glue and cover with green sparkles. Brush all the blue flowers and cover with blue sparkles. Repeat with each colour.

7 Attach flowers to cake using a little royal icing. Start with the large blossoms, then the leaves and finally the small blossoms.

8 Colour royal icing yellow and using a no. 2 piping nozzle, pipe a bulb of icing into the centre of each flower.

Wedding Cake

25cm (10in) & 15cm (6in) Marzipanned petal shaped rich fruit cakes, 20cm (8in) marzipanned round rich fruit cake, 33cm (13in) cake drum, 2.2kg (5lb) sugarpaste, Mexican paste, 350g (12ozs) modelling paste (p1), 20cm (8in) & 13cm (5in) thin cake cards, sugar glue (p1), Trex.

Squires Kitchen Paste Colours: Black, Forest, Rose, Gentian, Chestnut, Bulrush (hair colour).

Powder Colour: Snowflake Lustre, Rose.

Magic Sparkles: White x 2 pots ground finer (p1).

Bells & Bows cutter (PC), small blossom cutter (FMM), small piece of cotton net (if you cant get cotton nylon will do, but gathers will have to be stitched instead of glued), 2.4m (2½ yds) of beaded or sparkling ribbon, frilling stick / mouth tool, no.2 piping nozzle, 6 x plastic dowelling, pastry brush, glue stick, size guide (CC).

1 Place cakes on boards and ice. Ice board of bottom tier.

2 Push 3 dowel into 25cm & 15cm cakes. Mark with a pencil so you can trim them to be level with the cake surface. Remove each dowel, trim and return to cake. Place cakes in position so you can check they are level. If not, trim where appropriate and check again. When level, separate cakes.

3 Grease a non-stick rolling board and the large bell with Trex. Roll out Mexican paste thinly. Cut out bells and attach all over 15cm cake and on sides and over top curve of 25cm cake with sugar glue. Leave to dry.

4 Using a pastry brush, brush water thinly over 20cm cake but leave a centre 13cm circle dry. Also brush water over iced cake board. Leave both until 'tacky' then cover with white Magic Sparkles. Leave to dry.

5 Brush all bells with Snowflake Lustre.

6 Soften a little sugarpaste and using a no.2 nozzle, pipe a plain shell around base of bottom tier. Attach ribbon around cake board using a glue stick.

7 Place 20cm cake on top of 25cm cake, then the 15cm on top of the 20cm. Secure ribbons around cakes with softened sugarpaste (p1). Brush over bells and bows with Snowflake Lustre.

continued overleaf...

Wedding Cake

8 Roll a ball of white modelling paste to fit a size 15 on the size guide. Shape into a long cone for the brides dress. It should be approximately 6cm tall. Flatten top to take her head and pinch hem of dress to sit neatly on cake top. Secure with sugar glue.

9 Colour 60g of modelling paste grey. From a size 14 ball of paste, shape groom's trousers. Attach next to dress. Darken a little of the grey paste and shape shoes to attach to front of trousers. With white paste shape the front of the bride's shoes and attach.

10 Cut out a large bow from the bells and bows cutter and attach to front of bride's dress.

11 Colour 40g of modelling paste flesh using Rose and Chestnut paste colours. Roll a size 8 into a sausage 6¹/₂cm long (this is one long piece for both arms – you will not need to see any hands). Thin at each end for shoulders. Curve and attach to bride.

12 Take a size 12 ball of grey paste and shape for grooms body. Emboss a line with a knife and buttons with a piping tube on the lower half. Attach to trousers. Cut out a white triangle and attach to top half for shirt. Make a pale grey tie or cravat and attach. Cut out and attach a white shirt collar. Cut out grey lapels and attach.

13 Make 2 grey sleeves each from a size 8. Hollow out ends to take hands. Pinch at shoulders and mark creases at elbows with a knife. Roll two small balls of flesh colour paste for hands. Point at one end, brush with sugar glue and push up sleeve. Bend his right arm, attach at shoulder and hand on brides back. Brush hand and top inside of sleeve with sugar glue. Attach other arm.

14 Roll a no.12 ball of flesh for each head and attach. Emboss mouths with tool and dip a cocktail stick into black paste colour to mark eyes (the grooms mouth and eyes are embossed to the side). For groom's ears, flatten a small ball of paste, hollow out with a ball tool, then cut in half. Attach with sugar glue.

15 Colour a little sugar paste for hair, then soften with water (p1). Place in a piping bag, pipe onto heads and brush into style with a damp paintbrush.

16 Cut the tulle net to the required size of the veil. Keep it wider than the bride's head at the top so you can gather it slightly, then glue or stitch (see equipment list). Press veil into hair – pipe a little more hair if needed.

17 Colour a little modelling paste green, pink and blue. Attach a green teardrop shape over bride's hands. Mould some tiny green leaves and cut out approximately 14-16 blossoms. Attach flowers and leaves to bouquet headdress and buttonhole. Brush with a little sugar glue and add sparkles.

18 Add a little blush to cheeks with rose powder colour. Brush bride's shoes and bow with Snowflake Lustre.

Pram Cake

20cm (8in) Square marzipanned rich fruit cake, 31cm (12in) drum board, 1125g (2¹/₂ lb) sugarpaste, 225g (8ozs) royal icing (p1), mexican paste (p1), sugar glue (p1), Isopropyl Alcohol.

Squires Kitchen paste colours:
Violet, Mint Green, Blueberry, Rose, Chestnut & Black.

Powder Colour: Rose, Silver, Marigold.

Magic Sparkles: 2 x Hint of Green, 1 x White.

Wax paper or clear film, 7cm, 3cm & 2cm (3in, 1in, ³/₄ in) circle cutters (garrett frill centre cutters, piping tubes etc are ideal), frilling stick / mouth embossing tool (Jem), small blossom cutter (FMM), no.2 piping nozzle, pastry brush, sponge pad, paintbrush size 2.

1 For the pram, colour a little Mexican paste pale violet. Roll out thinly and cut out 7cm, 3cm and 2cm circles. From the 7cm circle cut out a quarter section. Place the pram body and wheels on a sponge pad to dry.

2 Colour a small piece of Mexican paste flesh using rose and chestnut. Roll out and cut out a 2cm circle. Trim the side and chin of the face to enable it to peep out of the pram.

Emboss a mouth with the embossing tool. Emboss eyes with a cocktail stick dipped into black paste colouring. Brush a little rose powder colour onto cheeks. If you would like the baby to have hair, place on wax paper and pipe or brush on a little coloured royal icing and leave to dry.

3 Trace pram pattern from p36 and cover with wax paper. Place the dry pram on to the wax paper. Colour a little royal icing grey and using a no2 piping nozzle pipe the pram handle. Now pipe over the pram handle, around the pram body and hood. Leave to dry. Pipe a bulb of royal icing in the centre of wheels.

4 Colour half of the sugarpaste pale mint green and half pale Blueberry. Ice the cake covering half in each colour, then the board.

5 Soften a little of the green sugarpaste with water (p1). Place in a piping bag and cut off the tip to approximately a size 2 piping nozzle. Take a good pinch of green sparkles and grind finer (p1). Pipe a line of sugarpaste along the join of the two colours (7cm at a time). Using a damp paintbrush, brush the icing up and down to resemble grass. Sprinkle the fine sparkles over this grassy edge. Repeat grass edge around base of cake (green area only) but do not use sparkles.

6 Using a pastry brush, brush water or sugar glue very thinly over green icing on cake, board and grass. When icing is 'tacky' sprinkle on the remaining whole green sparkles. Tip off excess.

7 Mix silver powder colour with isopropyl alcohol and paint pram handle, trim and wheel centres. Use a fine brush to paint a few spokes on pram wheels (optional). If you want to have the pram raised, attach small balls of sugarpaste with sugar glue underneath pram before attaching to centre of cake. Attach balls of sugarpaste under wheels before attaching to pram then attach baby's face straight to the cake, pushing down into the pram.

8 Cut out small blossom flowers (approximately 20 –30). Attach to cake with royal icing. Colour a little royal icing yellow and pipe a centre in flower.

9 Thin some royal icing with a little water and pipe cloud shapes straight on to cake. Allow to dry slightly then cover with fine magic sparkles (p1).

Fashion Birthday Cake

25cm (10in) Sponge cake, 33cm (13in) drum board, 1.3kg (3lb) sugarpaste, Mexican paste (p1), royal icing (p1), sugar glue (p1), jam and buttercream, Trex.

Squires Kitchen Paste Colours: Rose, Violet, Gentian, Mint.

Powder Colours: Snowflake Lustre, Silver.

Magic Sparkles: Hint of Pink, Hint of Blue, Hint of Lilac, Hint of Green, White, all ground finer (p1).

Small sharp knife, small blossom cutter (FMM), small heart cutter (FMM), Butterfly cutter (PC), Quilting (stitch) wheel (PME), no.1 piping nozzle, ³⁄₄in double curve serrated crimper, fine paintbrush, various small embossers ie flowers, hearts etc.

1 Half cake and spread with buttercream and jam. Place on board and cover thinly with buttercream. Roll out sugarpaste and ice cake. Ice the board and crimp the edge. Roll out long thin sausages of paste, attach around base of cake with sugar glue and crimp.

2 Colour Mexican paste in varying shades of pale colours. Cut out blossoms and hearts in appropriate colours.

3 Grease a non stick rolling board with Trex. Roll out pale blue paste. Grease small butterfly cutter with Trex and cut out 4 or 5.

4 Trace and cut out top patterns on p36. Trace the coat hanger.

5 Pipe message in centre of cake using a no.1 nozzle and royal icing. Mark coat hangers randomly over cake with either pencil tracings or a cocktail stick. Pipe with the no.1 tube.

6 Roll out Mexican paste thinly on a non-stick board greased with Trex and cut out different tops. Grease the top patterns with a little Trex to hold in place while cutting out. You can change the shapes of the neckline, sleeves etc as you cut out each one. Make each top different by embossing or using the stitch wheel. Attach each top over a coat hanger

with sugar glue. When dry either dust with Snowflake lustre or brush lightly with sugar glue and add magic sparkles.

7 Fill in gaps between tops with the blossoms, hearts or cut out some shoes and handbags(P37). Decorate as for tops.

8 Over pipe the crimped edges using a no.1 nozzle and royal icing. Pipe centre of blossoms.

9 Mix Silver powder colour with isopropyl alcohol and paint coat hangers and message. Paint butterfly antennae and centres of blossoms. Paint over piping on crimped edges.

Rabbits Cake

20cm (8in) Square marzipanned rich fruit cake, 28cm (11in) drum board, 900g (2lbs) sugarpaste, 450g (1lb) modelling paste (p1), a little royal icing, sugar glue.

Squires Kitchen Paste Colours: Gentian, Rose, Black, Mint.

Powder Colours: Rose, Snowflake.

Magic Sparkles: Hint of Blue, Hint of Pink, both ground finer (p1).

Straight frill cutter no.4 from set 1 (FMM), no.1 & no.2 piping nozzles, stamens, greaseproof paper, size guide (CC), frilling stick / mouth tool (JEM).

1 Place cake on board and cover with white sugarpaste.

2 Colour half the modelling paste pale blue.

3 Make a template from greaseproof paper for the side of the cake. It should be the length of one side and half the depth.

4 Roll out long strips of blue modelling paste. Place the template over and cut one long straight line. Place the frill cutter along the top edge of template and cut. Brush sugar glue around base of cake and attach blue strip.

5 Cut out a square of blue paste approximately 15cm using the frill cutter. Attach to top of cake with sugar glue. Roll out white modelling paste and cut out a 10cm square with the frill cutter. Attach to centre of blue square. Ice the board with the remaining blue modelling paste.

6 Brush all blue areas with sugar glue and cover with blue sparkles.

7 Using a no.1 nozzle, pipe a plain shell around base of cake in royal icing.

8 Colour a little royal icing pink. Pipe roses above side border and around blue square on top of the cake by piping a small spiral with a no.1 nozzle. Using green royal icing pipe a tiny leaf each side of the rose. When dry brush snowflake powder over roses and leaves.

9 The large rabbit is made from modelling paste using the size guide as follows:- Feet each a size 12, mark paws with a knife. Body size 14, mould a teardrop shape. Arms are each size 7, keep short, point at shoulders and mark paws with a knife. Head is a size 12. Mark mouth with a mouth tool and knife. Mark nose with a no.3 piping nozzle by tilting so you only emboss half of it. Cut three stamens in half. Cut ends off and push into cheeks. Dip tip of a cocktail stick in black paste colour and mark eyes. Ears are each a size 7, hollowed with a paintbrush handle. Attach a tail size 8.

10 Make small rabbit as large rabbit in the following sizes. Feet each a size 8, body size 11, arms each size 6, head size 8, ears size 5, tail size 6. Mould three tiny flowers and leaves from pink and green modelling paste and attach to hand.

11 Brush rabbits and centre white square with snowflake lustre. Dust rabbits nose and inside ears with a little pink powder colour.

12 Brush rabbits bodies with sugar glue and cover with appropriate colour sparkles. Attach rabbits to cake with royal icing.

Star Cake

20cm (8in) Round marzipanned rich fruit cake, 28cm (11in) drum board, 900g (2lb) sugarpaste, flower paste (SK), sugar glue (p1).

Squires Kitchen paste colour: Violet

Magic Sparkles: 2 x White, 2 x Hint of Lilac, Lilac.

5 White flower wires – size 22, star cutter set (FMM), single curve serrated crimper, No. 2 piping nozzle, posy pick, sponge pad.

1 Cut flower wires in half.

2 Roll out white flower paste thinly. Cut out six stars of each size plus an extra eight large (leave these eight on a sponge pad for the sides of the cake). Brush three small stars with sugar glue. Place a wire on each keeping the tip approximately half way down the star. Place a small star directly over the wire and first star.

3 Repeat with the medium size star placing 1cm below the small star, then with the large star.

4 Colour some flower paste pale violet and repeat the stars on wires. Colour some flower paste dark violet and repeat again. Cut out an extra eight small stars in dark violet (leave these eight on a sponge pad for the sides of the cake). Lay all stars on wires flat on a sponge pad to dry.

5 Place cake on board. Colour the sugarpaste pale violet then ice the cake. Crimp around the top edge of the cake.

6 Ice the board and crimp edge.

7 Grind one pot of hint of violet finer (p1). Brush side of cake with sugar glue. Sprinkle the fine sparkles over.

8 Soften a little sugarpaste (p1) and using the no.2 nozzle, pipe a small plain shell around base of cake.

9 Brush iced board with sugar glue and sprinkle hint of lilac whole sparkles over.

10 Brush stars for cake side with sugar glue and sprinkle with white sparkles. Attach small balls of sugarpaste behind stars with sugar glue before attaching to cake.

11 Fill the posy pick with pale violet flower paste and press into centre of the cake. Leave to dry slightly.

12 Grind each of the Magic Sparkles finer (p1). Brush one side of the stars on wires with sugar glue and cover with the appropriate colour sparkles. Leave to dry then turn over and repeat on other side. Leave to dry.

13 Push star wires into paste in posy pick. Bend slightly to give a curved shape.

Teddy Ballerina

20cm (8in) Square sponge cake, 28cm (11in) drum board, 900g (2lb) Shell Pink Regalice, Mexican paste (p1), royal icing (p1), sugar glue (p1), isopropyl alcohol, food colouring pen, rose (SK), jam and buttercream, Trex.

Squires Kitchen Paste Colours:
Cream, Rose, Violet, Black, Mint.

Powder Colours: Rose, Black, Snowflake Lustre, Silver.

Magic Sparkles: Pink, Purple.

Small star cutter (FMM), no.2 piping nozzle, paintbrush size 2, small sharp knife, 1m of marabou feathers.

1 Half cake and spread with buttercream and jam. Place on board and cover thinly with buttercream. Roll out sugarpaste and ice cake. Ice the board.

2 Trace teddy pattern from p34. Cut out pattern and place in the centre of cake. Mark the outline with a cocktail stick or knife (use a little trex on the back of the pattern to help keep it in place).

3 Cut each piece of the pattern out - keep the arms and head as one piece, also keep the legs and shoes together.

4 Colour a little Mexican paste cream for teddy, pink and violet for dress.

5 Roll out teddy colour paste thinly on a non-stick board greased with Trex. Grease the back of the head and arms pattern lightly and place on paste. Cut out and attach to cake with sugar glue. Repeat with dress pieces in appropriate colours. Cut the bows off the shoe pattern. Roll out the teddy coloured paste and cut out the leg with the shoe. Remove pattern and trim the foot area slightly. Attach to cake. Roll out shoe colour, cut out shoe and attach over foot area. Cut out bow and attach. Leave to dry.

6 Colour a little Mexican paste grey and cut out small stars. Attach to cake with sugar glue.

7 Colour a little paste green and pink. Mould small rosebuds by taking a ball of paste, rolling into a sausage, flattening and rolling up. Roll a ball of paste for a leaf, flatten, pinch and mark a central vein. Leave to dry.

8 Brush teddies head, arms and legs with snowflake lustre. Brush a little rose powder colour onto cheeks. Hold a piece of paper at edge of ear and using the same brush, brush from paper into ear. Remove paper and this gives a neat line of colour. Now repeat for snout but use a slightly curved piece of paper and a little black powder. Colour a little paste black. Mould eyes and a nose and attach to face with sugar glue. Draw a mouth with a food colouring pen.

9 Colour a little royal icing grey and pipe all outlines around and over bear. Leave to dry and then paint with silver powder mixed with isopropyl alcohol. Paint stars silver.

10 Brush iced board with a little water and cover with pink Sparkles. Paint sugar glue into pink part of tutu. Cover with Sparkles. Repeat with lilac part of tutu. Grind the lilac sparkles finer (p1). Brush bodice and shoes with sugar glue and cover with fine Sparkles.

11 Attach leaves and roses as a headdress using royal icing. Dust with snowflake lustre.

12 Trim marabou to fit around cake. Give it a good shake to remove any loose feathers. Attach to back of cake with a little royal icing (when feathers are removed cut the royal icing away).

Christmas Tree Cake

20cm (8in) Marzipanned rich fruit cake, 28cm (11in) drum board, 900g (2lb) sugarpaste, 225g (8ozs) Mexican paste (p1), royal icing (p1), Trex, Sugar glue (p1).

Squires Kitchen Powder Colours: Snowflake lustre, Fern.

Magic Sparkles: Hint of Green, White, Yellow, all ground finer (p1).

No.2 piping nozzle, Fern leaf cutter (FMM), Christmas Rose Corner (PC), Large Poinsettia, Holly, Ivy cutter (PC), ball tool, non-stick rolling pin & board, sponge pad.

1 Place cake on board and cover with sugarpaste. Ice board.

2 Soften a little sugarpaste (p1) and using a no. 2 nozzle, pipe a plain shell around base of cake.

3 Grease a non-stick board and the fern leaf cutter with trex. Roll out Mexican paste thinly – do not lift and turn. Cut out fern leaves. Remove surrounding paste then lift and place leaves on a sponge pad to dry. Cut out approximately 30 full leaves for the side of the cake.

4 Cut out fern leaves for the tree branches. You will need 6 full leaves for the lower branches. The tree has approximately 9 layers. As you cut out branches for further up the tree, trim them shorter. Cut out spares to allow for breakages. Leave to dry.

5 Grease a non-stick rolling board with Trex and roll out Mexican paste thinly. Grease the Christmas corner with Trex and cut out approximately 12 large roses. Grease the ivy and holly from the poinsettia set and cut out approximately 15 of each. Place on a sponge pad and soften edges with a ball tool. Leave to dry.

6 Dust all fern leaves for the side with snowflake. Brush thinly with a little sugar glue and sprinkle green sparkles over.

7 Shape a cone of sugarpaste approximately 10cm tall and 4cm wide at the base. Attach to cake. Starting with the full leaf at the base of the tree, brush a little sugar glue at end of leaf and push into cone at an angle 2.5cm up from the base. Continue around cone until you have 6 branches around base. If the stem on the leaf is too long to push in, snap off to a more suitable size.

8 Add next layer above (1cm) and between the branches below. Continue up the tree with branches getting shorter. As you work up the tree you will have less branches to each layer, finishing with approximately 3 on the top layer.

9 Dust centre of roses with a little fern powder colour taking it slightly onto the petals. Pipe a little royal icing roughly into centre. Dust over whole flower then leaves with snowflake lustre. Add a little sugar glue to centre of flower and add yellow sparkles.

10 Brush sugar glue randomly over flowers, holly and ivy leaves. Sprinkle green sparkle over leaves and white on flowers.

11 Using royal icing, attach roses, then ivy, holly and fern leaves around sides of cake.

Girls Birthday

25 x 20cm (10 x 8in) Sponge cake, 31 x 36cm (12 x 14in) drum board, 1.3kg (3lb) sugarpaste, 225g (8ozs) Mexican paste (p1), royal icing (p1), sugar glue (p1), Trex, coloured dragees (S.Cook), buttercream & jam, isopropyl alcohol.

Squires Kitchen Paste Colours:
Rose, Mint, Gentian, Violet.

Powder Colours: Snowflake Lustre, Silver, Rose, Gentian, Purple Mood, Fern.

Magic Sparkles: Hint of Pink, Hint of Green, Hint of Blue, Hint of Lilac, White, all ground finer (p1).

Balloon cutter (PC), Butterfly cutter (PC), No.2 paintbrush, flat dusting brush, No's 1 & 2 piping nozzles, large (25mm) and small (9mm) blossom cutters (FMM), Heart Cutter (20mm) (FMM), straight frill cutter no.5 set 2 (FMM), pastry brush.

1 Cut cake in half. Sandwich together with buttercream and jam. Place on board and mask with buttercream. Cover cake with sugarpaste. Ice board and emboss with frill cutter.

2 Knead 50g (2ozs) of Mexican paste into 225g (8ozs) of sugarpaste. Roll out thinly into long wide strips. Measure height and length of cake sides then cut a template from greaseproof paper. Roll out paste thinly and place template on top.

Cut one edge straight and the other with the straight frill cutter. Brush sides of cake with water. Roll up frill and unroll around the cake.

3 Grease a non stick board and the balloon cutter with Trex. Roll out Mexican paste thinly and cut out balloons. On the cutter there are three complete balloons to use individually. Place on a sponge pad to dry.

4 Brush sides of cake and down on to board to embossed edge with water using a pastry brush. When tacky sprinkle with white Magic Sparkles.

5 Place balloons on kitchen paper and dust with a flat brush. Brush from outside edge. Moisten a little in centres and cover with sparkles. Attach to cake sides with royal icing.

6 Colour a little mexican paste pale blue. Cut out two butterflies as for balloons and dry over folded card. Colour Mexican paste in appropriate colours and cut out 2 hearts, 2 large blossoms, 4 small blossoms. There is a pattern to follow for the bag, shoe and phone on (p35).

7 Enlarge the lettering for birthday (p35) on a photocopier to the required size. Trace and cut out. Roll out different coloured Mexican paste on a board greased with Trex. Put a little Trex on the back of each letter and place on paste to cut out. Place

each letter on a sponge pad to dry. When dry brush with sugar glue and cover with sparkles. Leave to dry. Position letters on cake and secure with sugar glue. Attach small blossoms into centres of B,d & a.

8 Place a no.2 piping nozzle in a bag and using royal icing pipe happy and name.

9 Dust blossoms, hearts, bag, shoe and butterflies with Snowflake Lustre. Attach to cake with royal icing. Attach balloons to side of cake and pipe a string using no.2 nozzle. Pipe a button and handle on bag. Attach dragees to centre of large blossoms.

10 Place a no.1 nozzle in a piping bag with royal icing and pipe the centre of small blossoms. Pipe a zig zag just above side border and on iced board close to embossed line.

11 Mix silver powder colour with isopropyl alcohol and paint zig zag lines, balloon strings writing, butterflies, blossom centres, phone and bag.

Teddy Ballerina (P28) 90% actual size

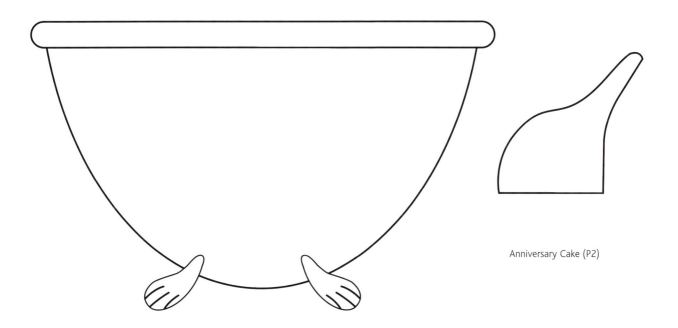

Anniversary Cake (P2)

Birthday

Girl's Birthday Cake (P32)

Fashion Birthday Cake (P22)

Pram Cake (P20)